THE PRESIDENTS AND THEIR PETS

By

VERA FOSTER ROLLO, PH.D.

Illustrations by Alvin C.

MARYLAND HISTORICAL PRESS

9205 Tuckerman
Lanham, Maryland

Copyright (c), 1994, Vera Foster Rollo.

Library of Congress Catalog Number 93-86023.

ISBN 0-917882-29-6. Hardback
ISBN 0-917882-36-9. Paperback

Printed in the United States of America.

First Printing 1994.

FOREWORD

Few things catch our attention as do pets — dogs, cats, ponies — and various other furry or feathered friends that live with us. The presidents of the United States and their families share this gentle mania with the rest of us, as this book will show. They have carried their pets along with them in horse-drawn carriages, on ships, in automobiles, planes and helicopters.

Learning about the animals that the presidential families cared for lets the young reader vividly see the presidents as people. This book should help young people remember the sequence of presidents, their names and some of their achievements. Yes, it is a good way to discover American history.

Knowing some facts about the presidents may entice young readers into libraries to learn more. The reader now can relate to the men who loved their pets. Presidents have found their pets to be friends that helped them relax, to bear the burdens and the loneliness of the presidency.

Let us go now to explore White House history and the stories of its denizens. It is hoped that this book may serve as an important footnote (paw print?) to American history for you.

Vera Foster Rollo
1993

iii

DISCOVERIES

While writing this book I came across four facts that would make grand "presidential pursuits" questions.

First, I noticed that there were two presidents named Harrison. There was the ninth president, William Henry Harrison, who served just 31 days, incidentally, in 1841 and there was his grandson, Benjamin Harrison, our twenty-third president, who served 1889-1893.

Second, two of our presidents were named Adams. The second, John Adams, served 1797-1801 and his son, John Quincy Adams, was the sixth president, who served 1825-1829.

Third, there were two presidents named Johnson. The seventeenth was Andrew Johnson, who served 1865-1869, and the thirty-sixth president was Lyndon B. Johnson, 1963-1969.

The fourth interesting fact is that there has been some dispute over the numbering of the presidents. This has happened because Grover Cleveland served twice. His first term was as our twenty-second president, 1885-1889. His second term was 1893-1897 as our twenty-fourth president. Is he to be counted once as one person? Or, counted twice as serving twice? (I counted him twice in this book.)

ABOUT DATES OF SERVICE -
AND TERMS OF OFFICE

Some confusion as to dates has occurred, due to the fact that the president is elected in a fall election but does not take office until the following year. Until 1933 our presidents took office on March 4th of the year following their election. This was understandable in the days of slow transportation. It did, however, leave the incoming president waiting in the wings for several months. And, annoying to the president leaving the office, he was termed a "lame-duck" (powerless) president.

Amendment Twenty to the Constitution of the United States, the "Lame-Duck Amendment," ratified by Congress in 1933 changed this. Inauguration Day for the president and the vice president was made January 20th. Further, the newly-elected members of Congress now were to begin each new Congress on January 3rd.

President Franklin D. Roosevelt was the first president taking office under these new terms.

Amendment Twenty also said that should a president die in office, the vice president would become president. After Roosevelt won a fourth term in office in 1944, Congress passed an amendment to the Constitution which said that presidents might serve at most, *two* four-year terms of office.

There are a lot of other details that you may want to look up about laws that regulate the Presidency. I won't delay longer here, however, but will get on with the tale of the White House pets and their owners.

Artist Alvin Jasper has hidden the "number" of the president in each illustration. For example, in President Washington's picture the number one is hidden somewhere in the picture and in President Clinton's picture you'll find the number 42 somewhere in the picture. They may be either numerical or spelled out. He believes you might enjoy finding these.

TABLE OF CONTENTS

Books by the same author

Your Maryland:
A History

The Proprietorship of Maryland:
A Documented Account

Maryland's Government

The American Flag

Henry Harford: Last Proprietor of Maryland

A Geography of Maryland

Maryland's Constitution and Government

The Black Experience in Maryland

Maryland Personality Parade

Burt Rutan: Reinventing the Airplane

Aviation Law: An Introduction

Aviation Insurance

Aviation Programs in the United States

GEORGE WASHINGTON

First President of the United States.

President 1789 - 1797.

Born: Westmoreland County, Virginia,
     February 22, 1732.

Died: December 14, 1799.

George Washington was chosen to be the military leader of the Americans who fought for independence from Britain in the American Revolution. He was then called General George Washington. After the Americans had won their freedom from English rule, he was elected by the Electoral College to be the first president of the United States under the new Constitution of the United States.* He took the Oath of Office of the President on April 30, 1789, in New York, New York.

At that time the White House had not been built. (It was begun in 1792 and completed in

1800.) President Washington and his wife Martha, for most of his terms, lived in Philadelphia. He was president for two terms, eight years. He longed to return to his home, Mount Vernon, on the Potomac River in Virginia.

Six cream-colored horses were used by George Washington to pull his coach. There were no automobiles then! Also, the family had a pet parrot, a cat and a dog. These pets moved along with the Washingtons from New York to Mount Vernon.

When at home at Mount Vernon George Washington joined his neighbors in fox hunts. In his blue coat, buckskin breeches, red waistcoat, wearing a velvet cap, off he would go with other riders galloping over fields, jumping fences and riding into the woods. He was an experienced horseman.

Washington bred horses at Mount Vernon. One of his stallions was named Magnolia. It was a beautiful Arabian. There were always dozens of horses on the farm.

A pack of hounds was kept at Mount Vernon. All had names. It is said that the first Basset Hounds came to America from France, a gift of the Marquis de Lafayette. Lafayette also sent a pack of large French hounds to Washington. These were snarling, tough dogs. They were also huge and fast. Mrs. Washington found this out one day when Vulcan, one of the pack, got into the kitchen, seized a whole ham and ran away with it.

There were many animals on the farm. There were mules, cows, sheep and pigs. There were also turkeys, geese and chickens. In addition to these domestic animals, many wild animals and birds lived in the fields and forests of the farm.

George Washington was very fond of his big white riding horse, Nelson. He had been mounted on this horse when he had accepted the surrender of the British at Yorktown, Virginia in 1781. He would have his grooms put a coat of white on the horse. When this whiting was brushed off, the horse gleamed. Also the horse's hooves were trimmed neatly and painted black.

Another horse that Washington rode many miles during the American Revolution was a tireless animal named, Blueskin. He was a strong, dark iron-grey stallion.

The capital city of the United States is named Washington in honor of our first president. It is located in the District of Columbia.

* John Hanson of Maryland has been called "Our Forgotten First President." This is because on November 5, 1781, he was chosen "President of the United States in Congress Assembled." He was our president under the Articles of Confederation. George Washington, however, was the first president of the United States to serve under the present Constitution of the United States.

JOHN ADAMS

Second President

President 1797 - 1801.

Born: Braintree, Massachusetts on October 30, 1735.

Died: July 4, 1826.

President Adams and his wife, Abigail, moved into the not-quite-completed presidential mansion in Washington, District of Columbia, (D.C.) in November 1800.

Adams was very familiar with animals. During his lifetime, horses provided the only means of transport, other than walking or riding in boats. Also, for generations his ancestors had farmed rocky fields near Braintree, Massachusetts.

John Adams studied law and joined in the fight for American rights. He was a supporter of the Declaration of Independence and served abroad as a diplomat for the new nation, the United States

of America. Adams served two terms as George Washington's vice president.

The Adams had a son, John Quincy Adams, who later served as president of the United States.

While president, John Adams had a stable built for the family's twelve horses near the presidential mansion. After leaving office, Adams retired to his farm in Quincy, Massachusetts.

Oddly enough, many years later, he and Thomas Jefferson died on the very same day in the year 1826. This was on July 4th, the 50th anniversary of the Declaration of Independence. The two men had a great deal to do with writing the Declaration.

THOMAS JEFFERSON

Third President.

President 1801 - 1809.

Born: Shadwell, Virginia, April 13, 1743.

Died: July 4, 1826.

At his Virginia home plantation, Monticello, Jefferson kept all sorts of wild fowl and animals. He liked to see them living on the land as peacefully as possible. There were many deer and rabbits.   There were also pigeons, squirrels, partridges and other wild poultry.

In his fish pond he kept trout, not as pets, of course, but for fresh food for his table.

A trained mockingbird was a special pet. He brought the bird along with him to the presidential mansion when he became president. The bird could imitate the calls of a cat or a dog. It also liked to sing when the president played his violin.

A cat shared the White House with Jefferson and had to be kept away from pet birds.

Jefferson had been a widower for 19 years when he became president. His wife's name had been Martha. They had had two daughters, Martha (Patsy) and Mary (Polly). During his terms of office his daughter, Mrs. Martha Randolph, sometimes served as his hostess.

When Jefferson moved into the presidential mansion he found the stables were not suitable for his horses. So, in 1806 he had new ones built. Also a cowshed was constructed and a clean, new carriage house. As you can see, the president's grounds were used to shelter many useful animals.

In 1803 Jefferson, by treaty with France, *doubled the size of the United States* by buying the huge Louisiana Territory.

When he left office, Jefferson retired to his beloved home, Monticello, near Charlottesville, Virginia. He lived there with his daughter Martha and her family, the rest of his life, busy with his many interests.

JAMES MADISON

Fourth President.

President 1809 - 1817.

Born: Port Conway, Virginia, March 16, 1751.

Died: June 28, 1836.

During the War of 1812, in the year 1814, President Madison was with American troops at Bladensburg, Maryland. He saw that the Battle of Bladensburg was being lost to the British advance. He sent word to his wife, Dolley, that the British were marching toward Washington and that she must quickly leave the city.

Among her hurried preparations to leave was the task of asking a neighbor to take care of her pet parrot. (After the British left the city, the parrot was returned to Mrs. Madison.)

When the British troops captured Washington, D.C. they burned the president's stables and carriage house. The president's mansion was also set on fire. When the British marched away, only the walls were left standing. When the building was later restored, the smoke-blackened walls were painted white. From this time on, the president's mansion was known as "the White House." A peace treaty was signed in 1815.

Upon retiring from office, Madison and his wife went to live at Montpelier, their country home in Orange County, Virginia. The parrot went along with them.

In fact, the parrot outlived the president. It stayed with Dolley Madison for many years in Virginia and later on in Washington, D.C. when she moved back to the capital.

JAMES MONROE

Fifth President.

President 1817 - 1825.

Born: Westmoreland County, Virginia, April 28, 1758.

Died: July 4, 1831.

    James Monroe attended the College of William and Mary in Williamsburg, Virginia. He joined the American army at eighteen and fought bravely in the American Revolution. After the war he studied law under Thomas Jefferson. He moved to Fredericksburg, Virginia, where he set up law offices.

    Monroe married Elizabeth Kortright by whom he had two daughters and a son (who died while still a baby).

    James Monroe became interested in politics and served as a United States senator. Later, he

was appointed Minister to France (1794-1796). He became familiar with the French people and their politics. This was to help him negotiate the vast land sale, the "Louisiana Purchase" which so greatly enlarged United States territory in Jefferson's term of office.

He is also remembered for the "Monroe Doctrine," a policy of the United States which restricted future colonization of the American continents by European powers. It was a "hands off" policy. It was during his Presidency that Spain ceded Florida to the United States. As you can see, Monroe added a great deal of land to the United States in his lifetime.

Monroe dealt with complex national and international matters before and during his presidency.

In addition to the family's cherished horses, the president's daughter Maria owned a small spaniel.

Monroe and his family retired to his country estate in Loudoun County, Virginia. He moved to New York City in 1830 after his wife died to be near his daughter, and lived there the rest of his life.

JOHN QUINCY ADAMS

Sixth President.

President 1825 - 1829.

Born: Braintree, Massachusetts, July 11, 1767.

Died: February 23, 1848.

John Quincy Adams began his public service at a very young age. When only 14, he went to Russia as private secretary to the United States Minister, Francis Dana. Dana was the first American diplomat in Russia.

Young Adams was the son of our second president, John Adams.

He became an attorney after graduation from Harvard College. With his early experience and with his training as an attorney, he was to serve the United States well in foreign service. By age 26 he was appointed the United States Minister to the Netherlands, then sent to serve with the Berlin Legation.

Adams was elected to the United States Senate in 1802, and six years after that appointed Minister to Russia. Later, serving under President Monroe, Adams was to be one of the country's greatest secretaries of state.

So it was an experienced leader who became president in 1825. During his term in office two strange White House "pets" were in the news. The Marquis de Lafayette stopped by to visit and with him was a gift alligator. Room was found for the scaly beast, but it was not adopted as a permanent pet by the president.

Silkworms, too, visited the White House. These had a brief stay on their way to other quarters. The idea of raising silk worms and beginning a silk industry was rather popular but also rather unsuccessful.

While living at the White House, President Adams liked to get up early and take a swim in the Potomac River. What did his wife think of this practice? Probably the charming Louisa Catherine Johnson Adams found this no stranger than many of the other adventures she had experienced as the wife of the busy Mr. Adams. They had met in London in 1794 and married three years later. She had followed him across war-torn Europe for years and then across thousands of miles of water to the United States.

After his term of office John Quincy Adams was elected to Congress in 1830 and (literally) spent the rest of his life there. In 1848 he suffered a stroke and fell to the floor of the House chamber. Two days later he passed away, after a long and extremely active life.

ANDREW JACKSON

Seventh President.

President 1829 - 1837.

Born: Waxhaw settlement, South Carolina, March 15, 1767.

Died: June 8, 1845.

Before he was elected president of the United States, Andrew Jackson (whose nickname was "Old Hickory"), had led an adventurous life. He had been a young lawyer in Tennessee, and had earned enough money to buy a plantation called the Hermitage near Nashville, Tennessee.

He was interested in thoroughbred race horses and raised these beautiful animals. Truxton, was one of these, a handsome bay who won races for him. Horses were a part of his life as he traveled as an attorney and as he served as a successful politician from Tennessee.

Jackson and his wife Rachel had no children of their own but cared for two boys and other children. A friend once stopped by the Jackson home on a chilly February evening. Jackson was sitting before the fireplace, alone but for a child and a lamb. It seemed that the child had cried because the lamb was out in the cold. Jackson had smiled and brought the animal in to please his little two-year-old adopted son, Andrew Jackson Hutchings.

He found his second ward, while taking part in battles on the Coosa River while on his way to Mobile on November 3, 1813. Fighting the Red Sticks Indians the American troops took prisoners, among them women and children. One of the children was a handsome three-year-old boy whose parents had been killed. Jackson sent him back to Huntsville and later took him to live at the Hermitage. There the Indian boy, Lincoyer, was raised with Jackson's adopted son.

While an officer in the War of 1812, he rode many miles leading his men. He became a Major General and was famous for winning the Battle of New Orleans against the British (January 1815). During his military service Jackson often rode a horse named Sam Patches.

After Jackson became president, but before his dear wife Rachel could move into the White House, she died. To help the president, Emily

Donelson, Rachel's niece, served as his White House hostess. She was married to another of the children the Jacksons had taken into their home, Andrew Jackson Donelson.

The Jackson family loved children. Jackson and his wife, and after her death, he and his relatives, raised many boys and girls, the children of relations and friends. Now where there are children there are pets. A variety of dogs, cats and other animals inhabited the houses the Jacksons used.

After his two terms as president ended, Jackson returned to Tennessee to live, comforted by the children he cared for and surrounded by scores of animals that were so much a part of everyday life at that time.

MARTIN VAN BUREN

Eighth President.

President 1837 - 1841.

Born: Kinderhook, New York, December 5, 1782.

Died: July 24, 1862.

Martin Van Buren was a short man, trim and erect. He liked to dress well. He was of Dutch descent and the son of a farmer and tavernkeeper.

Van Buren's wife, Hannah, was said to have been a pretty, gentle woman. She and Martin Van Buren were married in 1807 after Van Buren had begun his practice of law. The Van Burens had several children. Later, Hannah became ill and died in 1819. Van Buren did not marry again.

As a young lawyer, Van Buren had become interested in New York state politics. By 1821 he was elected to the United States Senate. Under Andrew Jackson he served as Secretary of State.

Called for his bargaining abilities the "Little Magician," Van Buren was elected vice president in 1832, and in 1837 became the president of the United States. He and his four bachelor sons moved into the White House.

The country had had a series of financial ups and downs, "booms and busts," and in 1837 a serious financial panic happened. Van Buren tried various things to improve the economy of the nation but nothing he did seemed to help. He was determined that the government be kept financially sound, so urged that even federal improvement projects be cut.

Van Buren was against the making slavery legal in new lands taken into the United States. So he managed to block the annexation (taking in) of Texas. Van Buren's presidency was a most difficult one.

There were happy notes, however, for his oldest son Abraham, met Angelica Singleton while living at the White House. Angelica was a relative of Dolley Madison. Abraham and Angelica were married in November 1828. After that, she served as White House hostess for Van Buren's term of office.

There were the usual horses used for pulling carriages and for riding kept on the White House grounds. Stable cats kept the mouse population down.

The president was presented with gifts while in office. Among these were two beautiful tiger cubs. (They were not kept at the White House very long!)

WILLIAM HENRY HARRISON

Ninth President.

President March - April 1841.

Born: Berkeley, Virginia, February 9, 1773.

Died: April 4, 1841.

"His Whiskers," was the name of the Harrison's pet goat. The president's grandchildren, Ben, his sister Mary and another granddaughter, Marcina, loved the animal. They liked to ride a small red cart around the White House grounds with "His Whiskers" harnessed to it.

To the president's dismay, one day he saw the goat running away with the red cart, Ben aboard. The old man rushed out to chase it, wearing his frock coat and a high silk hat, waving his cane. Finally he managed to reach the cart and rescue his grandson. Ben was unhurt and, in fact,

thought it a splendid ride!

The president and young Ben could not then see into the future and realize that little Ben would one day become the twenty-third president of the United States.

Near the White House were stables to shelter saddle horses and the horses used for pulling coaches and chaises. These horses were often much loved by their owners. Harrison rode a horse described as a "mean white charger" to the Capitol for his inauguration. Automobiles were far ahead in the future.

Also on the White House grounds was the president's cow, a Durham. She was kept to provide fresh milk for the White House table.

Anna Tuthill Symmes Harrison, the wife of the president, was not well at the time of his election. She delayed her arrival in Washington, D.C. Jane Irwin Harrison, widow of the president's son, came to the White House to serve as his hostess.

President Harrison was the first president to die in office. He served only 31 days before becoming ill with pneumonia. Mrs. Harrison never lived in the White House, and after the president's death, stayed at her home in North Bend, Indiana.

JOHN TYLER

Tenth President.

President 1841 - 1845.

Born: Near Greenway, Virginia, March 29, 1790.

Died: January 18, 1862.

      Tyler was born in Virginia and attended the College of William and Mary at Williamsburg, Virginia. He became an attorney. Politics interested him and he served as a Representative in the United States Congress and later was elected governor of Virginia.

      While he was president, Tyler's beloved horse died. The president ordered the animal buried at Sherwood, Tyler's home in Charles City County near Greenway, Virginia. On a marker the president had these words inscribed: "Here lies the body of my good horse, The General. For years he bore me around the circuit of my practice and all

that time he never made a blunder. Would that his master could say the same — John Tyler."

Tyler's wife, Letitia, was not well enough to entertain at the White House but lived a quiet life in the second-floor family quarters. Her daughter-in-law, Priscilla Cooper Tyler (whose husband was the president's son Robert), served as White House hostess. Sadly, Letitia died in the White House in September of 1842, the first wife of a president to pass away in the mansion. When Priscilla Tyler moved to Philadelphia in 1844, the Tylers' second daughter, Letitia Tyler Semple, served as First Lady briefly.

The first president to marry in office, John Tyler married Julia Gardiner, June 1844. After his term of office Tyler retired with Julia to his Virginia home, Sherwood Forest, where in the years that followed, several children were born to them.

In his last year, after 1861, Tyler helped create the Southern Confederacy. This was made up of a group of southern states whose leaders planned to secede from (leave) the union of the United States. Tyler was elected to the Confederate House of Representatives but died soon thereafter, during the Civil War.

JAMES K. POLK

Eleventh President.

President 1845 - 1849.

Born: Mecklenburg County, North Carolina, November 2, 1795.

Died: June 15, 1849.

     James Knox Polk was born in North Carolina but when he was about eleven years old his family moved to Tennessee. During his childhood he was not strong enough for rough games or farm work. He liked to read and to study. Not surprisingly then, later on he graduated with honors from the University of North Carolina.

     The young man took up the study of law. While working as an attorney, Polk became interested in politics and also became a friend of Andrew Jackson. He was nicknamed, "Young Hickory."

While serving in the Tennessee legislature, Polk married on New Year's Day, 1824, the dark-eyed and lovely Sarah Childress.

Soon Polk was elected to the United States House of Representatives. From 1835 to 1839 he was Speaker of the House. Later he ran for governor of Tennessee and was elected in 1839 for a two-year term. He was defeated in 1841 and in 1843 and it seemed his career in politics was over.

Sarah may have been glad to see him retire to work in Tennessee, for her husband's health was always a problem. But in 1844 Jackson proposed Polk as his choice for the Democratic party's next presidential candidate. Polk won the election. While president, in 1848, Polk added gas lighting to the White House. Prior to this candles and lamps had been used.

During Polk's administration the territorial expansion of the United States continued at a fast pace. Britain agreed to settle on the ownership of vast areas called the Oregon Territory. Other enormous amounts of land in Texas and California were in question. Through military force and by purchase, the United States acquired these huge land areas.

On retirement James and Sarah retired to a fine new home "Polk Place" in Nashville, Tennessee.

ZACHARY TAYLOR

Twelfth President.

President 1849 - 1850.

Born: Orange County, Virginia, November 24, 1784.

Died: July 9, 1850.

Zachary Taylor was a military hero before he was elected president of the United States. He had risen to the rank of General and was nicknamed "Old Rough and Ready." The horse he rode for miles, while directing many a battle and all through Mexico on one of his campaigns, was called "Old Whitey."

During his military years, both the General and his horse cared little for appearance. The General was rumpled and his horse shaggy. Only for parades did the two shine. Then the General would don a good-looking uniform and Old

Whitey, beautifully groomed, would prance along, almost in time to the music of the band. Whitey seemed to enjoy parades.

After being elected president, Taylor had the horse brought from Louisiana to Washington by sea. After the two old friends were reunited, the four-footed one was turned out to graze on the White House grounds. There are eighteen acres of land around the president's mansion.

Crowds of admiring citizens looked at the shaggy old horse through the White House fence. People liked to pull hairs from his tail for souvenirs! Whitey became quite famous and enjoyed his life. But when the Marine Band came to play he had to be tied up, for he would edge up to the musicians waiting for a parade to begin. Old Whitey loved parades.

Taylor's wife, Margaret Mackall Smith Taylor, called "Peggy," took little part in White House social events. Instead, she preferred to live quietly in the second floor family rooms. The Taylor's had three girls and a boy. The youngest daughter, Mary Elizabeth Bliss, served as White House hostess.

Just five days after attending the laying of a cornerstone for the Washington Monument, Zachary Taylor died, July 9, 1850, in the White House. The funeral procession on July 13th included the General's horse. The old animal was

groomed and shining. He walked in the procession as is the custom, riderless, with his master's boots turned backwards in the stirrups. It was a sad occasion, yet people watching had to smile as they noticed that souvenir hunters had plucked every hair from Old Whitey's tail. Even so, the sight of the animal brought tears to the eyes of many.

MILLARD FILLMORE

Thirteenth President.

President 1850 - 1853.

Born: Locke, New York, July 7, 1800.

Died: March 8, 1874.

    Fillmore was born in a frontier log cabin in the Finger Lakes area, in the state of New York. The boy worked on his father's small farm until he was fifteen.

    He attended a one-room school and later an academy. He fell in love with a pretty red-headed teacher, Abigail Powers. After some years, in which Fillmore studied law and became an attorney, they were married in 1826. Abigail Fillmore taught school for a while after her marriage which was unusual in those days.

    In 1828 the Fillmore's son Millard was born and in 1832 little Mary Abigail. By this time the

Fillmores were living comfortably in Buffalo, New York.

Millard Fillmore held state office and was for eight years a member of the House of Representatives. In 1848, while serving as Comptroller for the State of New York he was elected vice president of the United States. When President Zachary Taylor died in office in 1850, Fillmore became president.

He is noted for sending Commodore Matthew Perry to Japan in 1853 to meet with the emperor and begin trade with that country. Also, he helped pass the "Great Compromise of 1850" which tried to avoid conflict between our states over the question of slavery.

Abigail loved flowers and defended her gardens in New York and in Washington, D.C. against the prowling cats, dogs and chickens that threatened it. We don't know of any specific pets that were kept by the Fillmore family. Horses were kept in the White House stables for riding and for use as carriage horses.

Mrs. Fillmore liked books, music and a quiet life and so turned much of the work of being the White House hostess over to her attractive daughter Mary.

FRANKLIN PIERCE

Fourteenth President.

President 1853 - 1857.

Born: Hillsborough, New Hampshire, November 23, 1804.

Died: October 8, 1869.

Long before he was president, Franklin Pierce had come to Washington. During the 1830s he served first as a member of the House of Representatives and then as a senator for New Hampshire.

After serving in the Mexican War, Pierce was nominated for president and was to serve from 1853 through 1857.

Pierces' term began tragically for, before his inauguration, during a journey, the Pierces' 11-year-old son Benny was killed in a railway wreck in January of 1853. Jane Pierce, saddened by this

loss, lived quietly in the White House and turned much of the required entertaining over to a relative, Abigail Kent Means.

When Commodore Matthew C. Perry returned to the United States in 1855 from his historic "opening" of trade with Japan, he brought back many things from the exotic East that were new and strange to Americans.

Among his gifts to the president was a pair of "sleeve dogs." These were tiny, furry animals with blunt noses, large and protuberant eyes, and with bodies as small as the smallest of new-born puppies. The dogs were small enough to sit in the saucer of a coffee cup.

One of these was given to Pierce's Secretary of War, Jefferson Davis, and rode about Washington in the Secretary's pocket. The second dog stayed in the White House with the president and his family.

There were changes made to the president's mansion. It was Pierce who added the first installed bathtub to the family quarters in 1853.

While he was president he managed to keep the states from fighting over the question of slavery. He tried to buy Cuba from Spain but did not succeed. He did arrange to buy a narrow strip of land from Mexico. This was called the Gadsden Purchase. The land today forms the southwestern corner of New Mexico and all of southern Arizona.

JAMES BUCHANAN

Fifteenth President.

President 1857 - 1861.

Born: Near Mercersburg, Pennsylvania, April 23, 1791.

Died: June 1, 1868.

James Buchanan was tall, dignified and a very formal man. He was the only United States president who never married. He appointed as his official White House hostess his 26-year-old niece, Harriet Lane.

Harriet Lane filled the White House with flowers, fine art and people. She entertained graciously with many dinners, parties and other social events. She and the president made sure that handsome horses were available to pull White House carriages and for riding purposes.

Buchanan needed any distraction possible

from the very tense years of his administration. The various states of the union were quarreling over the question of slavery and other issues. During his final months of office, several states seceded (withdrew) from the union.

The president was not certain of his course of action. He did not believe that the states had a legal right to leave the union, but on the other hand he did not believe that the federal government had the right to prevent them from leaving.

His administration ended with no decision made. He handed the problems over to the next chief executive, Abraham Lincoln.
Buchanan was glad to retire with his niece to his Pennsylvania home, Wheatland. (Later, Harriet Lane was to marry a banker from Baltimore and they were to have two sons. In her later years she returned to Washington, D.C. to live.)

Buchanan took many memories away from the White House with him. In May 1860, for example, when the colorful Japanese trade mission had come to the city to visit. He was, however, glad to be home in Pennsylvania, during the years that the tragic Civil War was fought.

ABRAHAM LINCOLN

Sixteenth President.

President 1861 - 1865.

Born: Hardin County, Kentucky, February 12, 1809.

Died: April 15, 1865.

The Lincolns had a dog, but the pet did not get to live in the White House. Fido was a dog, not with two tails, but with two homes. He was a "shared" black and yellow-brown pooch of unknown ancestry who tagged after Willy and Tad, Lincoln's sons. Fido also spent time with the Roll boys who lived nearby. When Lincoln was elected president, Fido was left behind in Illinois.

The three Lincoln boys were named Robert Todd, Willie and Tad. Mischievous and bright, the children were adored by their parents. Visitors, however, found them not always

51

delightful. In fact, Tad sometimes threatened visitors with the wrath of his pet goat. The Lincolns gave their boys a cat and a dog.

Ponies were bought for the boys to ride on the White House grounds and beyond. There were no automobiles yet, but there were plenty of horse-drawn vehicles.

Sadly, on February 20, 1862, death visited the White House when little Willie Lincoln died of a fever, probably typhoid. His pony was kept, in memory of him, in the White House stables.

Tad was so sad, after Willie's death, that people tried to cheer him up by sending him pets. A pair of soft, pink-eyed rabbits arrived. Then a pair of goats arrived and these did make him smile. He named them Nanny and Nanko.

To tell the truth, Tad took a goat upstairs with him where it slept on his bed. When President Lincoln was told about this, he laughed and would not send the goat away.

In the summertime the Lincoln family sometimes retreated from the heat and dust of Pennsylvania Avenue to a hill where the Soldier's Home was located. Lincoln allowed the goats to ride there in the presidential carriage along with the family.

Mrs. Lincoln (Mary Todd Lincoln) did show annoyance, however, when goats arrived in her living room or the kitchen.

On February 10th, 1864, President Lincoln looked out of the White House window and saw that the stables were on fire. He raced out to save Willie's beloved pony but was too late. (Horses in a burning stable, you know, often refuse to leave. They must be blindfolded and led to safety.)

There were plenty of pets left at the White House and Mrs. Lincoln called the president's cats "his hobby." It seemed to help Lincoln relax a moment to sit on the floor and play with them gently. Shortly after he had taken office, the Civil War had broken out. (Civil War, 1861 - 1865.) As it raged on, there were many heartbreaking decisions to make. Lincoln had decided to use military force to try to bring the seceding states back into the union of states.

A flock of pigeons, pets of Tad Lincoln, proved to be all too successful. To this day, efforts continue to control the flocks of birds that spatter buildings in the capital city.

White House history was made, in a light hearted way, when the Lincoln cat had kittens and the dog had puppies on the same day.

Other birds and animals lived on the White House grounds. There was Tad's turkey, "Jack." And there was "Old Bob" the family horse.

In his second term of office, as the Civil War was ending, President Lincoln and his wife attended a performance at Ford's Theater in

Washington, D.C. It was Friday, April 14, 1865. He was shot by John Wilkes Booth and died the next day.

It has been said that, with him died the possibility of peace with generosity after the Civil War.

ANDREW JOHNSON

Seventeenth President.

President 1865 - 1869.

Born: Raleigh, North Carolina, December 29,
1808.

Died: July 31, 1875.

    Just as the Civil War was ending, President
Lincoln was murdered at Ford's Theater. Vice
President Andrew Johnson became president.
    His were difficult years as president. He
tried to rebuild the United States and heal the great
anger and sorrow of the Civil War. He and the
Congress could not agree on ways to do this. The
ruined southern states were placed under military
rule.
    Congress passed the Civil Rights Bill of
1866 which made black persons citizens and
forbade discrimination against them. Congressmen

agreed that no longer could a government take away any person's liberty, life or property without "due process of law." (The Fourteenth Amendment to the Constitution.)

Johnson's wife, Eliza, was deeply loyal to her husband. She with members of their large family, lived on the second floor of the White House and took little part in the social life of the city. Her daughter Martha Patterson often served as hostess.

When there are children and grandchildren about, there are generally plenty of pets. In troubled times, it is helpful to admire a beautiful horse, a devoted dog, or even a fluffy kitten. There is, in fact, a story that the president befriended a family of mice!

The Johnsons survived the turmoil of their White House years and returned to Tennessee.

ULYSSES S. GRANT

Eighteenth President.

President 1869 - 1877.

Born: Point Pleasant, Ohio, April 27, 1822.

Died: July 23, 1885.

Grant began life on a frontier farm in Ohio.
As a boy he seemed to have an almost mystic affinity with animals. Some claimed that he could communicate with them without speaking. When only eight years old, his father gave him the money to buy a colt. He raised the horse and all his life never lost that love for horses.

His hard-working parents wanted their son to have more education than they had been able to get. He went to school until he was nearly seventeen years of age.

Then he attended the U.S. Military Academy at West Point, New York. He was noted not so much for his grades as for his excellent riding skills. Remember that at this time there were no automobiles, aircraft or tanks. Animals provided much of the motive power for the military services. There were railroads, however, by this time, with steam-powered locomotives.

After graduation in 1843, Grant served in the Mexican War and at various posts. In 1848 he married Julia Dent. The Grants had four children. Six years later he resigned from the military and tried one job after another with little success. With the outbreak of the Civil War, Grant was appointed a colonel, and later became a general, in the Union army. In the years 1863, 1864 and 1865, he planned and led successful military operations against the Confederacy of Southern States.*

During the war he rode a frisky black horse that he named "Davis." (The president of the Confederacy was Jefferson Davis.) Another horse that he used was "Cincinnatus," given to him early in the war by the citizens of Cincinnati, Ohio.

He had the reputation of being a hard man, pressing his soldiers forward, it seemed, almost without regard for the cost. When the Confederate forces surrendered to him at Appomattox, Virginia, however, he showed compassion by letting the soldiers of the southern army keep their horses to ride home and to use to work their farms. Grant wrote generous terms of surrender that would prevent trials for treason. The southern states were devastated and Grant may well have felt that the people had suffered enough.

War hero Grant was nominated in 1868 by the Republican party as their candidate for president. He served two terms of office, from 1869 to 1877. During this time, in 1873, the country suffered from a deep economic depression.

Grant brought to the White House his two horses, Davis and Cincinnatus. The latter was used as a model for the statue of the president on his horse which was placed in front of the U.S. Capitol. Five other horses shared the stables. There was a team of bay horses, called Egypt and St. Louis, used to pull carriages. The president kept a racing mare, Julia. Nellie Grant, daughter of the Grants, owned two mares, Jennie and Mary, used for riding. There were also two Shetland ponies, called Reb and Billy Button for the Grants' sons, Jesse and Ulysses, Jr. ("Buck").

Other horses came and went, for the president loved trotters and racers. He would often drive out with a trotter harnessed to a buggy. One day while out driving, he noticed a fast-moving delivery wagon. He followed the wagon and learned that the horse belonged to a butcher. Grant admired the animal and bought it, naming it "Butcher's Boy."

Jesse also brought to the White House a

parrot, an ill-tempered bird as it turned out. The boy also kept game cocks but was more interested in dogs. One of his favorite playmates was Faithful, a beautiful Newfoundland.

Later in his life Grant, the hardened soldier, was said to have turned away in pity and distress from tiger-hunting in India and bull-fighting in Mexico.

For two years after leaving the White House, Grant toured Europe with his family. Returning to the United States he found his business affairs in poor shape and his funds low. Suffering from cancer he worked hard to complete writing his *Memoirs* so that his family would have money from its publication to live on after his death. Grant died soon after its completion. He is buried in an elaborate tomb in New York City.

*In recent years it has come to light that a military planner of great ability from Maryland, assisted Grant with his Tennessee Valley campaign strategy, Miss Anna Ella Carroll. She had worked with Lincoln in Washington and later went west to Grant's headquarters to propose various plans that were later successfully carried out by Grant and his men.

RUTHERFORD B. HAYES

Nineteenth President.

President 1877 - 1881.

Born: Delaware, Ohio, October 4, 1822.

Died: January 17, 1893.

Rutherford Hayes won the closest and most debated presidential election yet held. Hayes, a well-educated attorney had served as a Union major-general in the Civil War, had been a member of the House of Representatives and also had served three terms as governor of Ohio. Yet, in spite of his experience, in the fall of 1876 he went to bed on election night believing that he had lost the election for president. Indeed, the vote was so close that it was months before the matter was decided.

Once made president, Hayes was recognized for his fairness but realized that the stresses and hatreds of the Civil War lingered. He tried to protect the rights of black citizens in the country, but also wanted to return peaceful, local self-government to all of the citizens of the southern states. By April 1877 the last federal troops were to leave the south. Yet there was still much to do.

Hayes, his wife Lucy and their children arrived in 1877 to move into the White House. Keeping up with modern innovations, by 1879 President Hayes had telephones installed in the mansion.

Washington, D.C. was really little more than a country town in the late 1800s. It was routine that the White House fields had pens of chickens. Hayes also kept pedigreed Jersey milk cows on the grounds. There were stables for the horses.

There were pets, too. Goats were used to pull little carts. The White house menagerie also included various dogs and a cat, plus several pet birds, including a tame mockingbird.

Hayes is recognized for his honesty and his efforts to operate an honest government. He had promised to serve only one term as president. So when the term was over, he and his family, with their pets, returned to their estate, Spiegel Grove, at Fremont, Ohio.

JAMES A. GARFIELD

Twentieth President.

President March - September 1881.

Born: Cuyahoga County, Ohio, November 19, 1831.

Died: September 19, 1881.

President Garfield achieved success in life by ability and hard work. His father died when he was only two years old. As a boy he worked at driving canal boat teams and managed to earn enough money for an education.

After his graduation from college he became a college professor and a college president. He was elected to the Ohio Senate in 1859. Later he fought in the Civil War with the Union army. He rose to the rank of brigadier general and then major general of volunteers. Meanwhile the people of Ohio elected him to Congress. At the urging of

President Lincoln, he resigned from the service and came to Washington. He served in the House of Representatives for 18 years.

Nominated for president, he won the election of 1880.

In 1881 he, his wife Lucretia and their children moved into the White House. It was a cheerful family. Lucretia gave receptions and dinners.

Horses were kept by the president for his use and for his family to use. His little daughter Molly had a horse named Kit. As was the custom for women, she rode Kit sidesaddle. One day the saddle slipped and Molly fell. She was dragged, screaming, her foot caught in a stirrup, until rescued. Amazingly she was unharmed. She lost her interest in riding after this incident.

President Garfield was very much determined to run an honest government and to get rid of people appointed more for favor than for ability. This made him many enemies. A man who had wanted to be appointed to a consular post but was not, shot the president in July 1881. Garfield lingered for weeks. He was taken to the New Jersey shore to recuperate, but died there in September 1881. His wife and family returned to their farm in Ohio.

CHESTER A. ARTHUR

Twenty-first President.

President 1881 - 1885.

Born: Fairfield, Vermont, October 5, 1829.

Died: November 18, 1886.

     Chester Arthur taught school after graduation from college. Then he studied law and became an attorney. He met lovely young Ellen Herndon in 1856 and they were married in 1859.
     The Arthurs' two children were given many toys and treats as Arthur's law practice prospered.
     In January of 1880 Chester Arthur's beloved wife Ellen died. He grieved for her the remainder of his life.
     He was a very successful attorney and politician. At that time there was a "spoils system." The political party in power believed that it had the right to put people, who had worked and

voted for the party, in jobs in the government. Arthur at that time saw nothing wrong in this. He was nominated for vice president in 1880 and served in that office under President Garfield in 1881.

When Arthur became president, following the tragic death of Garfield in 1881, he changed his mind. He saw that it was unfair to hire or fire people in government jobs just because they worked for one political party or the other. During his administration he helped install a bi-partisan Civil Service Administration that made government hiring and firing less political.

When Chester Arthur became president, his son was seventeen years old and his daughter only ten. Arthur asked his youngest sister, Mary Arthur McElroy, to help with the care of his little daughter. She also supervised entertaining at the White House. Arthur had the White House redecorated and held many receptions and dinners there.

In 1885 President Arthur attended the dedication of the Washington Monument. He could look back upon his term of office and see that he had helped get more modern ships for the Navy, had improved the postal service and worked for honest government.

We are still looking for a specific pet living at the White House but with a little girl there, there were surely pets! Automobiles were still some years in the future, so horses were still kept in the White House stables for pulling carriages or buggies and some were used for riding.

GROVER CLEVELAND

Twenty-second President *

Twenty-fourth President

President 1885 - 1889.

President again 1893 - 1897.

Born: Caldwell, New Jersey, March 18, 1837.

Died: June 24, 1908.

By the time he was twenty-two, Grover Cleveland had become an attorney and became very successful. He was elected Mayor of Buffalo, New York. He ran such an honest government there that he was next elected governor of New York State.

When he became president in 1885, he continued his policies of honest government. This did not please some people, but it did please many

voters!

Cleveland was married to the beautiful, young, Frances Folsom, in the White House, June 2, 1886.

Mrs. Cleveland enjoyed the company of a pet mockingbird and several canaries while in the White House.

There was a concern around 1886 that several North American animals were facing extinction. In March of 1887 William Temple Hornaday, taxidermist and collector of animals, working for the new National Museum, proposed that the Smithsonian Institution begin a National Zoological Park in Washington.

The next October, a "little try-out zoo" was opened on the Mall. There the public flocked to see living American animals, mule deer, bison, prairie dogs, badgers, lynx and a few exotic birds.

Mrs. Cleveland and her husband gave a Golden eagle (a Christmas present) to the zoo in December 1887. The Clevelands also decided not to keep at the White House a beautiful little white tailed deer fawn. This began the practice of donating unwanted White House animals to the zoo.

Congress, in the years that followed, voted to locate a national zoo in Washington. Its goal was to preserve American birds and animals from extinction. In March 1889, President Cleveland signed the bill for obtaining land in the Rock Creek area of Washington for the National Zoological Park.

Frederick Law Olmsted developed a plan for the park which is only now being realized. On April 30, 1891 the zoo opened to the public. Not only native animals but those from around the world were housed there. A circus lent animals during their off-season and scores of birds and animals were donated.

While at the White House, Mrs. Cleveland received a little black "Japanese poodle," said to be the smallest "pug dog" in the country. It weighed only one-and-one-half pounds. Actually it is thought that the dog was neither pug nor poodle but probably a Lhasa Apsos or perhaps a Pekingese from China.

In the next presidential election, Cleveland received more popular votes than his rival, but lost the election in the electoral college vote. As Mrs. Cleveland left the White House she told the staff, "I want everything just the way it is now when we come back. That will be in exactly four years!" She was right. The Clevelands returned to the White House in 1893 for another term of office. With them was their baby daughter, Ruth. Two other daughters were born to the Clevelands, while they lived at the White House, Esther in 1893 and Marion in 1895.

President Cleveland left the federal government a reformed one upon his retirement from office. The Clevelands went to live in New Jersey at "Westland," where two sons were born to them and where you may be sure, there were plenty of pets for the family to enjoy.

* Some lists of the presidents of the United States name Grover Cleveland only once as the twenty-second president. Recent lists give him two numbers as we have here. This is the reason that from Grover Cleveland on, the presidents may have different numbers! Some lists count William McKinley as the twenty-fourth president.

BENJAMIN HARRISON

Twenty-third President.

President 1889 - 1893.

Born: Near North Bend, Ohio, August 20, 1833.

Died: March 13, 1901.

Our twenty-third president and our ninth president were related. Benjamin Harrison was the grandson of William Henry Harrison our ninth president.

Benjamin Harrison was born in Ohio and served in the Civil War on the Union side. He is reported to have been a dignified, little man with a cold manner. Others, however, said that he was a warm, kind-hearted man. His great-grandfather had been a signer of the Declaration of Independence and had served as a governor of Virginia.

Ben was raised on a farm in Ohio and was seven years old when his grandfather was elected

president. He was a good student and became an able public speaker. He went to Cincinnati, Ohio, to study law and became an attorney.

When only nineteen years old, and before completing his studies, he married his college sweetheart, Caroline Scott, in 1853. In the years to follow, they had a son and a daughter. Ben and his wife moved to Indiana where he was quite successful and popular. When the Civil War broke out, Ben served as an officer in that tragic conflict.

Later Harrison served in the Senate (1881 - 1887). Nominated for president by the Republican Party, Harrison had less popular votes than his opponent, but won the Electoral College vote over President Cleveland.

Harrison's wife, Caroline, moved into the White House in 1889. Harrison's daughter, Mary McKee, the two McKee children and other relatives, also lived at the White House. Mrs. Harrison entertained a great deal at the president's mansion. Sadly, in 1892 she became ill and died at the White House. Mrs. McKee acted as her father's hostess for the rest of his term.

Several horses were stabled at the White House and used for transportation. With young children at the mansion several cats, dogs and ponies were there.

The Harrison's grandchild, toddler Benjamin Harrison McKee, also called by reporters, "Baby

McKee," was shown in newspaper photographs driving his goat cart, riding in a pony card and talking to his dog.

We have learned that President Harrison decided not to keep a raccoon at the White House! He donated the animal in April of 1890 to the National Zoo. Two opossums, "Mr. Reciprocity" and "Mr. Protection," followed the raccoon to the zoo in June 1892. A peafowl was donated by the president to the zoo in February 1893. These "pets" were found on the White House grounds or given to the chief executive as gifts during his term of office.

President Harrison added electricity to the White House in 1891, but is said to have refused to turn on the newfangled electric lights himself. He was afraid of being shocked.

On leaving the White House, Harrison returned to the practice of law and married again in 1896.

WILLIAM McKINLEY

Twenty-fifth President.

President 1897 - 1901.

Born: Niles, Ohio, January 29, 1843.

Died: September 14, 1901.

All his life, McKinley said, he had never
been in doubt that he would someday be president!

Born and raised in Ohio, he went to college
a short time, later enlisted in the Union army and
fought in the Civil War. He left the service with
the rank of Major.

After the war, McKinley studied law and
began a law practice in Canton, Ohio. He met and
married Ida Saxton. They had two children but
both of these died young.

In line with his ambition, McKinley ran for
Congress and was elected. He served in Congress
for fourteen years and became a leading

Republican Party member. In 1896 he was nominated for president. Refusing to leave his wife (who was not well) to get votes, he ran a "front porch" campaign. McKinley won the election with a large majority vote.

Mrs. McKinley, never robust, moved into the White House with her husband and with courage attended the social events there. The couple were very devoted to each other.

A "Mexican double-yellow-headed parrot," as it was described, was President McKinley's favorite pet. Quite a remarkable bird, it could sing as well as talk!

President McKinley, in the records of the National Zoo, is credited with donating to the zoo two raccoons (1900) and two opossums (1901).

During the McKinley administration the Spanish-American War took place, with fighting begun and ended in the year 1898. The Treaty of Paris was signed, ending the war officially and shifting the ownership of several territories. Spain gave the United States Guam, Puerto Rico and the Philippine Islands. Spain was paid twenty million dollars for the Philippines. Cuba was declared an independent nation and Spanish forces left the island.

During the Spanish-American War, on July 7, 1898, Hawaii became United States territory.

Peace returned and all seemed to be well

with McKinley. In 1900 he was elected to a second term as president. Business was good in the United States. There was a big fair in Buffalo, New York, in 1901. McKinley went there to visit. While he was shaking hands with some of the people there, a man stepped forward and shot the president. The killer said that the reason he did this was that he wanted to kill a great ruler and was against government! Eight days later McKinley died.

McKinley's vice president, Theodore Roosevelt, became president.

THEODORE ROOSEVELT

Twenty-sixth President.

President 1901 - 1909.

Born: New York City, October 27, 1858.

Died: January 6, 1919.

    While not exactly pets, very noticeable inhabitants of the White House were animal heads placed on the walls of the State Dining Room by President Roosevelt. He really was a big game hunter, but actually most of these heads had been bought from a New York decorator!

    With Theodore and Edith Roosevelt, six Roosevelt children moved into the White House. (Edith Carow and Roosevelt had married in 1886.) There was Quentin, 3; Archie, 7; Ethel, 10; Kermit, 12; Ted, 14; and Alice who was 17 years old. (Alice was the daughter of Roosevelt and his first wife, Alice Lee, who died in 1884.)

Along with the family, a virtual zoo of animals arrived, too. There were three dogs — a small black mongrel called Skip, a Chesapeake Bay Retriever called Sailor Boy and Kermit's terrier, Jack.

Skip slept on the foot of the president's bed. When out on hunting trips, poor Skip would get tired. Then the president would scoop him up and let him ride with him on his horse.

Skip also liked to ride a pony. Algonquin was Archie's small Icelandic calico pony. The docile animal would gallop around the White House lawns and let Skip jump up on his back. Algonquin was mischievous. He liked to quietly come up behind people and push them with his shaggy little head.

The president was a most active man and loved to ride in all kinds of weather. One of his favorite horses was a huge animal called Bleistein. Riding horses kept were called: Renown, Rusty, Gray Dawn, Root, Jocko, Yagenka and Wyoming. The carriage horses were named Judge and General.

Roosevelt had been born to a wealthy New York family. He graduated from Harvard University. Soon he was deep in politics and became known as an honest reformer. He served in the years that followed in many government posts. Roosevelt became a hero of the

Spanish-American War. Later he was elected governor of New York State. In 1900 he was nominated for vice president. With McKinley's death, he became president.

More dogs were to join the White House menagerie. One of these was burly Pete, a bull terrier of uncertain temper. And then cats, Tom Quartz and Slippers! Slippers had six toes and liked to wander off for days, returning to attend White House parties! Tom Quartz loved to bedevil poor Jack, the terrier. No matter how hard Jack tried to hide, Tom would find him and jump onto his back.

But this was not all! There were guinea pigs, turtles, hens, rabbits and an occasional lizard. There were snakes, a parrot and a horned toad. For a while there was even a grouchy bear, called Jonathan Edwards.

At the "Summer White House," Sagamore Hill, at Oyster Bay, Long Island, New York, more animals shared the Roosevelts' lives. At one time or another one could meet a lion, a hyena, an eagle, a zebra, a wildcat and a number of other animals, birds and reptiles. When one of these pets grew too big or too dangerous to keep, the National Zoo in Washington, D.C. gained a resident.

The children spent a lot of time one summer trying to fit a one-legged rooster with a wooden leg, but nothing really worked. Indeed he got along very well, hopping about on his one leg. The White House children were sometimes tempted to be mischievous to gain attention. Quentin, for example, liked to carry snakes around in his pocket and display them unexpectedly.

Quentin brought four snakes home from a pet shop, one day, and dropped them onto a table in the Oval Office where his father was meeting with several important people. The senators and other guests leaped to their feet. Roosevelt and his son apologized and recaptured the squirming reptiles. The snakes were taken, rather quickly, back to the pet shop.

Alice liked snakes. Her favorite was a little green one named Emily Spinach. Whether her very thin Aunt Emily liked having a snake named for her has not been recorded. The "spinach" part of the name, Alice said, was because the snake was green. Occasionally Alice took Emily Spinach along on visits to her friends.

A badger named Josiah was acquired in Kansas when a little girl pushed him onto the platform of Roosevelt's train. (In those days, before cars and airplanes were commonly used, presidential candidates "whistle-stopped" in trains, stopping to make speeches from the rear platform.)

Alice outgrew the snakes but not her fondness for pets. She returned from a trip to the

Orient with a spaniel, called Manchu, given to her by the Empress of China. "Princess Alice" married Nicholas Longworth in a beautiful White House wedding.

While their father was attending to many presidential duties, including working toward making the Panama Canal a reality, the Roosevelt family led an active life in the White House. One day Archie had the measles and felt lonely, kept to his bed. His brother Quentin went out to the stables and led Archie's pony, Algonquin, into the White House, into the elevator and along the second floor hallway to Archie's room!

Theodore Roosevelt had been a skinny little boy with many problems with his health. He learned to love being out of doors and through exercise and fresh air had become healthy and strong.

He was a leading naturalist and a prolific writer. He liked to list the dozens of wild birds that lived in the trees around the White House.

National Zoo records show that President Roosevelt donated forty animals and birds to that institution. Among various American fauna such as opossum, squirrel and raccoon, there were also lynx, a black bear, a badger, and a coyote. Also, somehow, a goat was sent along to the zoo.

Gifts from around the world were gratefully received and, probably just as gratefully, passed on to the National Zoo. These included an eight-month-old Abyssinian lion in 1904, also, Somali ostrich, zebra,lion and baboon in 1904 (presented by the King of Abyssinia). In 1905 a jaguar (yes, the animal, not the automobile) was passed along to the zoo. Two Golden eagles were given to the zoo in the years 1904 and 1905 by the Roosevelts.

After leaving the White House Roosevelt went back to his Long Island home where he continued with his writing. He continued to travel and to work toward political reform. Wherever he lived, he was surrounded by his family and with a swarm of birds and animals.

WILLIAM HOWARD TAFT

Twenty-seventh President.

President 1909 - 1913.

Born: Cincinnati, Ohio, September 15, 1857.

Died: March 8, 1930.

Since automobiles were beginning to take the place of horse-drawn carriages, President Taft converted the White House stables into a garage. He installed his White Steamer, two Pierce Arrows and a Baker Electric automobile.

Animals, however, were not completely banished, for the automobiles shared the garage building with the Taft's milk cow, Pauline. Pauline was a stately Holstein. Taft is remembered as the president who kept his cow on the White House lawn!

Also, horses were kept for riding. The president liked to ride for exercise. His horse certainly must have been a strong one, for the president weighed over 300 pounds!

William Howard Taft was a good lawyer and had a successful practice in Ohio. He married Helen Herron in 1886. In 1887 the governor of Ohio appointed Taft to the state supreme court. Then in 1901 Taft was appointed civil governor of the Philippines, which then belonged to the United States. Mrs. Taft went there to be with him, with their three children, Robert, Helen and Charles.

President Theodore Roosevelt recognized Taft's ability and appointed him Secretary of War. Later, Taft ran for president.

When elected president, Taft tried to carry on Roosevelt's reforms of the civil service and set up coal and oil reserve lands. Actually Taft did not enjoy being president with all the pressures and politics it involved. He was happier later, his term over, when he became a professor of law at Yale University. When he was appointed Chief Justice of the United States Supreme Court he had found the work he loved. He served on the Supreme Court until he retired due to ill health, in 1930.

Taft's wife, Helen, proved to be a brilliant White House hostess. The famous Japanese cherry trees were planted around the Tidal Basin at her request. She continued to entertain well, too, during Taft's years as Supreme Court Chief Justice.

WOODROW WILSON

Twenty-eighth President.

President 1913 - 1921

Born: Staunton, Virginia, December 29, 1856.

Died: February 3, 1924.

    "The animal heads must go," said Mrs. Ellen Wilson, looking over the State Dining Room of the White House after her husband's election, "they are positively gruesome." So it was that these particular White House "pets" installed in Theodore Roosevelt's time, were removed. The heads were stored (where else?) in the Smithsonian Institution.

    The Wilsons and their three daughters kept several dogs at the White House. Wilson's wife kept pet canaries, as well. Sadly, Ellen Wilson died in August 1914. The Wilson's daughter, Margaret, took over the duties of White House

hostess.

President Wilson married again in December 1815. His second wife's name was Edith Bolling Galt. She took over the duties of White House hostess.

Animals were news and the press gave considerable attention to a flock of sheep that Wilson kept to raise wool and to keep the lawns mowed. This was during World War I (which began for the United States in 1917).

The flock of sheep was made up of thirteen ewes and Ike, a ram. Ike liked to chew tobacco. He learned to beg for it and was cross when not given his "chew." Unfortunately the sheep not only nibbled the White House grass but ate many expensive bushes and flowers, as well. The wool was auctioned off, however, and raised quite a lot of money for the American Red Cross.

After the war ended in 1918, the flock by now seventy sheep strong, was given away to L. C. Probert, a bureau superintendent of the Associated Press. He kept the sheep on his farm near Olney, Maryland.

Strange animals and birds wandered onto the White House grounds or were presented to the president. The National Zoo received from the president in the years between 1913 and 1918 a horned lizard, four opossum (one an albino), a South American ocelot, two bald eagles and a domestic turkey.

Edith Wilson was not only an able White House hostess, but also, she aided her husband as much as she could as his health declined following a stroke in 1919. She brought matters to his attention and was his constant attendant.

In 1921 the Wilsons retired to a comfortable home in Washington, D.C.

WARREN G. HARDING

Twenty-ninth President.

President 1921 - 1923.

Born: Near Marion, Ohio, November 2, 1865.

Died: August 2, 1923.

When only 16 years of age, Harding moved into Marion, Ohio, and there found that he liked newspaper work. He managed to buy the small *Daily Star*.

Later he met Florence Kling De Wolfe. Soon they married and built a house in Marion. This was to remain their home for the rest of their lives. Mrs. Harding had a son by her first marriage but no children with Warren Harding.

Harding was active in many business and social organizations in Marion and became interested in politics. He was elected to several offices before being elected president.

After moving into the White House in 1921, many photographs of the president on the front pages of newspapers showed him walking with his dog, Laddie Boy.

Caswell Laddie Boy was a small, shaggy, Airedale — with his own social calendar and his own chair! The dog even attended cabinet meetings with the president and had a chair there.

Mrs. Harding had a lively sense of fun and entertained often at the White House. Neighborhood dogs were once invited to Laddie Boy's birthday party. (The cake was made of layers of dog biscuits topped with icing.)

On May 11, 1921, Laddie Boy seated on a float, led a parade in honor of the Humane Education Society. The Smithsonian Institution owns a statuette of Laddie Boy.

Another dog, Oh Boy, lived at the executive's mansion. He was an English bulldog and escorted the president and Mrs. Harding on strolls about the grounds.

The Hardings decided to pass on to the National Zoo several gifts in 1921 and 1922. These were an Alaskan bald eagle, an opossum, a coyote, and a Virginia opossum.

There was a pen for turkeys kept (outside) at the White House and there were canaries caged inside the mansion.

The president often had to be away from

Washington. Mrs. Harding went with him when she could. On one of these trips, a journey to the Pacific coast in July of 1923, Harding became ill and died. Mrs. Harding sadly arranged for funeral services and then directed the move from the White House.

Laddie and Oh Boy waited for their master's return, but they did not see him again.

CALVIN COOLIDGE

Thirtieth President.

President 1923 - 1929.

Born: Plymouth, Vermont, July 4, 1872.

Died: January 5, 1933.

Grace, President Coolidge's wife, loved her husband's white collie so much that she had her portrait painted with the dog. She is shown, by the artist Howard Chandler Christy, with Rob Roy on the south lawn of the White House. She is wearing a red silk dress in the painting. Mrs. Coolidge was a beautiful, dark-eyed woman.

Mrs. Coolidge enjoyed her canaries, Nip and Tuck. She also had a white canary from California, called Snowflake and a thrush called Old Bill. One year, just for fun, at the annual White House Easter egg rolling, she dressed all her dogs in Easter bonnets. Even Rob Roy wore a

dashing black veil!

The collie was originally named Oshkosh for the town he came from, Oshkosh, Wisconsin, but Mrs. Coolidge changed his name. In due time a mate for Rob Roy was purchased, Miss Prudence Prim, a lovely white collie with soulful eyes. She was not a robust dog but was a very loving one. In 1926 Miss Prim died and two years later Rob Roy, too, passed away.

When they learned of the Coolidge's loss of their dogs, two children in Michigan sent a replacement, a Shetland sheepdog called Diana. Mrs. Coolidge changed Diana's name to Calamity Jane. Jane was a happy and playful animal and loved to chase Mrs. Coolidge's grouchy chow dog, Tiny Tim. Tim was a medium-sized brownish-red dog.

Other Coolidge dogs were Ruby Rough, a brown collie; a small bulldog called Beans; King Kole, a black police dog; Palo Alto, a trained bird dog and Bessie, a yellow collie.

Calvin Coolidge was a lawyer in Massachusetts. It was in Massachusetts that he entered politics. He worked his way up to become governor of Massachusetts. Calvin and Grace were married in 1905. They had two sons, John and Calvin, Jr.

When President Harding died, in 1923, his vice president, Calvin Coolidge, became president.

After serving out Harding's term, Coolidge was elected for another term of office. During his administration the White House was renovated extensively.

Pets continued to come in. The president was fond of Rebecca, a raccoon from Mississippi. A pen was built for her near his office. She was joined by Horace, another raccoon, but only briefly. No romance ensued, since Horace climbed out of the pen and vanished.

A pair of lion cubs were given to the president by the mayor of Johannesburg, South Africa. These were not kept but were sent along to the National Zoo. Coolidge sent the zoo quite a few gifts: a pygmy hippopotamus, a donkey, an antelope, a clutch of chickens, a white goose, a bald eagle, a peafowl, a bobcat, a lynx, a duiker from South Africa, a wallaby (a kind of kangaroo) and a black bear. The Coolidges also parted (gladly) with an alligator in 1926.

During the summer of 1924 the Coolidge's son, Calvin, Jr., became ill and, like Willy Lincoln sixty years earlier, he died despite all efforts to save him. The White House, like any other family home, has had many happy times and sad ones, too. The Coolidges carried on, in spite of their sorrow, until the end of the president's term in 1929.

Mrs. Coolidge was a charming woman who

helped her husband with her winning ways. He was a very quiet man, often called "Silent Cal," by reporters.

It is said that President Coolidge adopted a stray cat, or perhaps the cat adopted the president. Its name was Tiger. It came to the White House and took "Silent Cal" for its master. Another cat, Blacky, stayed at the White House for a time. He had to be penned up, however, for he liked to hunt birds and squirrels.

Laddie Buck, a half-brother to President Harding's dog, Laddie Boy, was also a pet of the Coolidge family. He pushed his long and beautiful nose into everything. Mrs. Coolidge changed his name to Paul Pry! He couldn't be trusted not to bite, however, so ended up in the care of the U.S. Marine Corps, the only outfit tough enough to control him, some said!

Another of the Coolidge dogs that didn't last at the White House was Peter Pan, a wire-haired terrier. He, too, was too unfriendly to keep. There were plenty of pets left, however, and only by donating gift animals to the National Zoo were their numbers kept within limits!

HERBERT HOOVER

Thirty-first President.

President 1929 - 1933.

Born: West Branch, Iowa, August 10, 1874.

Died: October 20, 1964.

     King Tut was President Herbert Clark Hoover's dog, his friend and his faithful guardian. In fact, King Tut, a Belgium police dog, became known as the "dog that worried himself to death!"
     Hoover became King Tut's master while Hoover was in Belgium in 1917, working as a war relief organizer.
     Hoover and his wife Lou, married in 1899, and led an adventurous life in the years before returning to the United States. A mining engineer, Hoover and his family had lived and worked in China, Ceylon, Burma, Siberia, Australia, Egypt, Japan and had visited several countries in Europe.

During these years, two sons, Herbert and Allan were born to the Hoovers.

The youthful millionaire was recognized for his work organizing war relief efforts during World War I. He was also known for his writing. He and Lou decided to build a home in Palo Alto, California, but Hoover was appointed Secretary of Commerce and so they moved to Washington for eight years. In the early 1920s, Hoover, his family and the dog lived on S Street Northwest in Washington, D.C.

By 1929, Herbert Hoover was elected president and moved into the White House. King Tut's life changed. Many strangers were coming and going and King Tut worried. He kept as near his master as he could during the day, sleeping lightly, always alert. It was his duty to pick up the morning newspaper and bring it to the president. When the president sat out of doors to read the news, King Tut sat on the papers to keep them from blowing away.

At night he prowled the White House fence, checking that the guards were in place, trying to find out which ones were familiar and getting acquainted with new guards. Hoover tried to keep his faithful pet in at night, so that King Tut could get some rest. But the dog would bark and whine until released to his night patrols.

As the president's term went on, King Tut,

growing older also grew more anxious and restive. In fact, it was not safe for workers to enter the rear grounds. Tut grew thin and grouchy. It was obvious that he was a danger to those around the White House that he didn't know.

Finally, when all else failed, he was sent back to the Hoover's S Street house, where he had been happy. The dog pined away and died. The burdens of the Presidency were just too much for him. His faithful heart could not stand the strain of trying to protect his master under conditions that the poor animal could not understand. President and Mrs. Hoover did not release the news of King Tut's death right away. Mr. Hoover had no heart for another dog right away. Also, the country was in a dark mood because of the terrible stock market crash of 1929 and a deepening economic depression.

Allan, the Hoovers' son, brought other pets to the White House. He kept two dogs, two cats, and added two ducks. Then two alligators were donated to the president and Allan was delighted. His parents were not. They insisted that during the night the alligators be kept in a bathtub and not left to wander the great house in the darkness!

National Zoo records show that the Hoovers gave the zoo an American alligator in 1929, (Allan's pet?) and a red-shouldered hawk in 1930.

Among the White House dogs of the Hoover

administration were little white fox terriers, Big Ben and Sonny. There was a pair of large wolfhounds. These were so large that tourists looking through the fence sometimes mistook them for ponies.

Briefly there was Yukon, an Eskimo dog. Also there was Eaglehurst Gilette, a magnificent setter. Mrs. Hoover's special pets were Weejie, a playful small elkhound and a police dog called Pat. She featured these two on her 1932 Christmas cards.

And then there was the 'possum. It arrived on its own one spring and was mentioned in the newspapers. The president donated the little animal to a school baseball team in Hyattsville, Maryland, as a good luck mascot. It seems that the ball team had recently lost *their* opossum. Was it the same one? No one knows. It is known that the team did well that year!

In 1933 the Hoovers retired to Palo Alto, California.

FRANKLIN D. ROOSEVELT

Thirty-second President.

President 1933 - 1945.

Born: Hyde Park, New York, January 30, 1882.

Died: April 12, 1945.

In many photographs of President Roosevelt we can see there beside him a small, black Scotty with fuzzy, pointed ears, named Fala.

When President Roosevelt took his first look around the White House he noticed that the kennels were in an area that would get quite hot in the summer. So, he decided that his dogs would not be kept there but allowed to roam the house and grounds. Fala added to the dog count by fathering two pups, Meggy and Peggy.

The president owned a large, black German shepherd called Major, a handsome dog with buff markings. Major had a habit of taking a visitor's hand in his mouth and holding on for what seemed to the visitor to be quite a long time! Later the protective big dog bit several visitors and so had to be kept in a doghouse. He was sent home to Hyde Park after biting a senator.

Mrs. Eleanor Roosevelt often walked her little Scottish terrier, Meggie. This dog sometimes slept in fireplaces, which meant that she frequently had to be bathed. Meggie, too, was guilty of biting strangers. She is said to have nipped a reporter on the nose. The White House is a nerve-racking place for people and also for dogs! In any event, Meggie had to go.

Winks was another canine "nipper," but forgiven because he seemed to bite playfully. The young Llewellyn setter was a mischievous and happy dog.

One day, walking past the kitchen, Winks noticed nineteen plates of fragrant bacon, toast and eggs sitting on the table. It was breakfast for the domestic staff. The chef had stepped out of the kitchen for a moment. When he returned, he found that Winks had cleaned every plate. When the president heard about this, he laughed and said that someone should have poured Winks some coffee, too.

Winks died young, in the summer of 1933, while playing with another dog on the White House lawn, happy to the end.

Franklin D. Roosevelt, "FDR," was born, like his fifth cousin, former President Theodore Roosevelt, to a wealthy family and attended fine colleges. FDR married Eleanor in 1905. They were to have six children, one of whom died as an infant. FDR entered politics and held several offices. In the summer of 1921 disaster struck when FDR contracted the dread disease poliomyelitis, "polio," as it was known. No vaccine was available at the time.

With great courage Roosevelt struggled back to health. He would never regain the strength he formerly enjoyed, but he greeted cameras and visitors with a cheerful smile. In November of 1932 he was elected president, to the first of four terms. (After his administrations the laws were changed to permit only two terms as president.)

During his terms of office the Great Depression finally came to an end, World War II was fought, and many new government social programs were installed. So many new agencies were set up that some said all their initials made quite an "alphabet soup"!

When Franklin Roosevelt, Eleanor and their children moved into the White House for their long stay, it became a most lively mansion. The National Zoo served as overflow receptor for some of the gifts the president received, taking on pigeons, dove, a serval (African wildcat), a caracal (lynx), rabbits, alligators and an African hedgehog.

For a time a Great Dane, named president, lived with FDR. The dog that became the most famous, however, was the Scotty, Fala. Roosevelt was given the puppy in the spring of 1940. It proved to be love at first sight and forever. Fala slept by the president, played near the office window and faithfully turned up for cocktail hour.

Fala loved to ride in the president's car. Everywhere FDR went, little Fala went — to Warm Springs, Georgia, to Hyde Park, New York. The president's paralyzed legs were eased by the warm waters of the Georgia spa. Hyde Park was his family home.

In fact, Fala even went along on important conference trips as World War II continued its grim course (1941-1945). He was a close and furry companion to the president as they traveled many thousands of miles by sea and by surface transport.

As World War II was drawing to an end, one April day in 1945, Fala sat watching his master posing for a portrait, when suddenly FDR fell forward. The artist rushed to help the president. Doctors hurried in, but nothing could be done. The nation mourned the death of their president.

A quiet little Fala went to live at the Roosevelt family home in Hyde Park, New York.

The president's widow, Eleanor Roosevelt often took the dog on trips with her. Fala lived with Mrs. Roosevelt for another seven years. Then, in another April 1952, Fala died and was buried in the rose garden at the Hyde Park estate.

HARRY S. TRUMAN

Thirty-third President.

President 1945 - 1953.

Born: Lamar, Missouri, May 8, 1884.

Died: December 26, 1972.

When President Roosevelt died, Harry S. Truman, vice president, became president. This was only a very few months after Roosevelt had taken on his fourth term of office. Suddenly, the complex duties of leading a nation still at war were given to Truman.

Truman had grown up in Independence, Missouri, and had earned a good living as a farmer in Missouri for twelve years. He served in World War I and was a captain in the Field Artillery. After the war he came back to Missouri, married Elizabeth "Bess" Wallace and opened up a men's clothing store.

Interested in politics, soon Truman was elected a judge in Jackson County and became a United States senator in 1934. He became Roosevelt's vice president in 1945. Truman served out Roosevelt's uncompleted term and in the next presidential election was elected for another four years.

When President Truman and his wife, with their daughter Margaret, moved into the White House, Truman had much to face. He had difficult, terrible, decisions to make in order to end the war. There were hard choices to make to try to work for world peace and to rebuild nations hurt by World War II.

Mrs. Truman, too, found hers a difficult task, doing required entertaining in a mansion that had serious flaws. The old house was showing its age, not just on its surfaces but in its underpinnings, too. In their second term of office the Truman family had to move into Blair House, across the street from the White House, so that extensive repairs could be done to make the chief executive's house safe and comfortable to live in.

Margaret Truman took voice training and was interested in writing. She wrote a book about some of the pets that had lived in the White House. Later, after her marriage, she was to further develop her interest in writing. She has become a most successful author.

Margaret's dog was an Irish setter. The president for his part, befriended a squirrel, and a friendly mixed-breed dog.

He decided not to keep two gifts, an albino kangaroo and a bird-of-paradise, attractive as they were. He sent these along to the National Zoo in 1952.

President Truman did not to run again and in 1953 retired with his family to his home town of Independence, Missouri.

DWIGHT D. EISENHOWER

Thirty-fourth President.

President 1953 - 1961.

Born: Denison, Texas, October 14, 1890.

Died: March 28, 1969.

    A brown Weimaraner, Heidi, shared the White House with President Dwight D. "Ike" Eisenhower and his wife Mamie. Heidi seemed to think that the president of the United States belonged to her. She even tried to keep Mamie away from Ike.

    Heidi had a delightful life, often riding in a limousine to the president's farm in Gettysburg, Pennsylvania. David, the president's grandson, sometimes visited the White House with his little Scottish terrier, Spunky.

    Ike loved golf. He enjoyed practicing on the White House putting green. The local squirrels, too, liked to play and dig on the green. So, Capital Parks Service maintenance crew members caught and carried bagsful of surprised squirrels away to distant parks.

Eisenhower was a career military man. Born in Texas, he was raised in Abilene, Kansas. As a young man he received an appointment to West Point. After graduation, Ike was sent to a post near San Antonio, Texas. There he met young Mamie Doud. They were married in 1916. The couple lost their first child, a son, but another son, John, was born to them in 1922.

Ike served in the peacetime army and many years later became a general. Eisenhower was placed in Europe and helped lead the United States forces in Europe to eventual victory in World War II. After the war he retired from the military and served as president of Columbia University. Later, he served as commander of the newly established, North Atlantic Treaty Organization.

In February 1952 he was asked to run for president. Elected that fall, Eisenhower served two terms in office. The Eisenhowers were able to move into the just-renovated White House.

The president needed all the relaxation he could get from pets and golf, in the complex eight years of his presidency. What was called the "cold war" was in progress. Relations between nations were tense. The threat of nuclear war was a continual concern. Ike worked to reduce world tensions.

At home, Eisenhower continued programs designed to further the cause of racial equality and the desegregation of schools. He ordered that the nation's military services be completely desegregated. Also, Ike stressed the need for a balanced national budget.

The Eisenhowers decided against keeping at the White House several beautiful gift animals: a pair of Korean bear cubs, fourteen Alaskan reindeer and an African forest elephant named Dzimbo. These were donated to the National Zoo.

President Eisenhower owned a canary called High-Glory, and a parakeet who could not talk, unfortunately named Gabby.

After leaving the White House, Ike and Mamie retired to their farm in Pennsylvania. Their son John and his wife Barbara came to visit them there, often bringing along the four grandchildren. There was a lot for children to do and see on the farm. There were broad fields, woods; there were pet dogs, riding horses and several prize Angus cattle.

JOHN F. KENNEDY

Thirty-fifth President.

President 1961 - 1963.

Born: Brookline, Massachusetts, May 29, 1917.

Died: November 22, 1963.

Born to a large and wealthy family, John Fitzgerald Kennedy, as a young man, attended Harvard University. After graduation, he joined the Navy and served in World War II in the Pacific. Home again, recovered from combat injuries, Kennedy was elected to the House of Representatives and later, to the Senate. He married beautiful Jacqueline Bouvier in 1953.

In 1961, John Kennedy (JFK as he was known) and his wife Jackie with their two children Caroline and John, moved into the White House. Caroline was three years old and John was just two months old.

Both children were taught to ride ponies. In the summer when the family visited Cape Cod, Massachusetts, they liked to ride about there in a little cart pulled by one of the ponies.

Caroline's pony was called Macaroni and John's, Leprechaun. A third pony, Tex, was given to the children by Vice President Lyndon Johnson. Tex proved to be a wild little animal and gave the White House animal caretakers many a tussle.

In the winter, Jacqueline took the children for rides in a horse-drawn sleigh on the south lawns of the White House.

Another equine pet was a bay gelding, Sardar, a beautiful horse, given to Mrs. Kennedy by the president of Pakistan. He also offered her an elephant and some tiger cubs but these she politely declined!

Jackie loved animals. An expert horsewoman, she rode as often as possible. She also liked to take, Clipper, their German shepherd, with her in her station wagon. She liked to take the big dog for runs in nearby parks.

Dogs! Yes, many dogs were pets of the Kennedy family. Grandfather Kennedy gave Caroline a little Welsh terrier, that she named Charlie. Charlie was to enjoy living in the White House. He loved to join the president in the White House pool! (Kennedy often swam to strengthen the muscles in his sometimes troublesome back.)

But, dogs and ponies were only a part of the White House animal-bird-and-fish collection during the Kennedy years. There were ducks, rabbits, goldfish, the parakeets Bluebelle and Maybelle, hamsters (Debbie and Billie) and a canary called Robin. The hamsters escaped into the air ducts of the White House on one occasion, emerging in the president's bathroom.

There was a gray cat, with yellow eyes, too. His name was Tom Kitten. The president was allergic to cat fur, however, so a good home had to be found for Tom.

The Kennedy's were given a dog in 1960, named Pushinka. This in Russian means "fluffy." It was given by the Premier of Russia, Nikita Khrushchev. Pushinka was the daughter of the Russian space-traveling dog, Strelka.

Pushinka moved into the White House with the Kennedys and Charlie became her mate. When Pushinka had puppies, the president called them "pupniks," a play on the word "Sputnik." (The Russian Sputnik was the satellite that had astonished the world when it had been launched, October 4, 1957, by the Soviet Union.) Jacqueline had made a nest of shredded newspapers for Pushinka so that the puppies would be warm. The "pupniks" were duly named Blackie, Butterfly, White Tip and Streaker.

Now this increased the dog population

considerably, so to find good homes for two of the puppies, Jackie Kennedy sponsored an essay contest for children. The essay was to tell how, if the writer won a puppy, how the dog would be treated. Thousands of letters poured in and finally two pups were awarded to two happy children.

Pushinka was a willing dog and bright. She learned to climb a ladder up to Caroline's tree house and then slide down a chute on the other side.

Another White House dog was Shannon, born 1963. It was given to the president by the prime minister of Ireland. It was an Irish cocker spaniel. Later, an Irish priest sent the president a huge wolfhound, Wolf (or Wolfie). (The Kennedy family was descended from people who came to the United States from Ireland.)

One day Caroline's pony, Macaroni, wandered over to the office window and looked in at President Kennedy. They stared at each other for a moment and then the president opened the door and invited Macaroni in. She thought about it for a bit, but then turned and walked away.

Macaroni's decision was a wise one, for the president in that Oval Office during his "1000 days" of office had to contend with many serious matters. There was the war in Vietnam, the Cuban missile crisis, a treaty to reduce the testing of nuclear bombs, the problem of the Berlin Wall that divided Germany, and many other items to think about.

The president went to Dallas, Texas in November of 1963 and was killed there by an assailant. The entire nation mourned the loss of this young and popular president. The author remembers that day. She heard the news on her car radio and later saw Maryland school children walking home. They were crying for him.

It was then up to lovely, young Jacqueline Kennedy to return to Washington, attend last services, comfort Caroline and John. She had to arrange to gather up and move the Kennedy belongings, the children and the multitude of pets.

LYNDON B. JOHNSON

Thirty-sixth President.

President 1963 - 1969.

Born: Near Stonewall, Texas, August 27, 1908.

Died: January 22, 1973.

Lyndon Baines Johnson, born on a ranch, worked his way up in life. He held many jobs and eventually earned his way through college. His parents had both been school teachers and both his grandfathers had served in the Texas legislature. He grew up with a respect for learning and a liking for politics.

After teaching for a time, Johnson came to Washington, D.C., where he worked as secretary to an influential Congressman from Texas. During this time, while visiting his home state, Johnson met a young lady, Claudia "Lady Bird" Taylor. Just two months after they met, they were married

in November of 1934.

Lady Bird invested money she had inherited in a radio station and being a good businesswoman, she eventually earned several millions of dollars. The Johnsons had two daughters, Lynda Bird and Luci Baines.

Lady Bird helped her husband with his political career. Johnson was elected to Congress as a member of the House of Representatives (1937) and, several terms later, to the Senate (1948). While he was away in the military and again away (1955) to recover from a heart attack, Lady Bird could be relied upon to help with his work.

In 1961 Lyndon Johnson was sworn in as President Kennedy's vice president. When Kennedy was murdered, Johnson became president on November 22, 1963.

The Johnsons arrived at the White House a simple two-dog family. Their beagles were named Him and Her. Soon, however, a schoolgirl in Illinois sent the president a handsome, white collie, named for the Spanish word for "white," Blanco. The dog turned out to have more beauty than brains, but the president loved him.

Long before he became president, Johnson, often called "LBJ," was a beagle fancier. He had Little Beagle, originally his daughter Luci's dog, for years. Little Beagle doted on his master, the then senator from Texas. When LBJ was ill, the dog insisted on climbing onto his bed to comfort him. LBJ returned the dog's affection. When Little Beagle died of old age he was buried on the family ranch back in Texas.

Lady Bird Johnson as First Lady, soon set to work on programs for the beautification of the capital city. The work she began soon spread across the country. She supported her husband, as well, with his work for the Head Start program and his programs for civil rights and many social programs to assist young people (education) and older citizens (social security).

Imagine, a wedding in the White House! And it was a beautiful one when Lynda Bird married Charles Robb.

LBJ, fond of animals, liked to have his dogs with him. They went along on cruises of the presidential yacht, in limousines and aircraft. The president liked to look in on them in their quarters located near the flower room at the White House. The beagle, Her, died in 1964. The surviving beagle, Him, went on to become a father of roly-poly puppies, Edgar, Dumpling, Kim, Little Chap and Freckles. Only Kim and Freckles were kept. The others were given away to good homes. Active to the last, Him died in 1966, struck by a car while chasing a squirrel.

There is a 1966 United Press photo of Johnson cradling beagle puppies in his big hands, with the beagle "mom," Freckles, looking on. Having his pets around him seemed to help the president withstand the worry and stress of his work. The Vietnam War, for example, went on and on with heavy losses.

When on his Texas ranch, LBJ liked to call an old buck deer, George, to his car. The president would reach out and feed him.

Another dog, Yuki, arrived to cheer the White House occupants. Yuki was small and white. Luci found him at a gas station in Austin, Texas. No one claimed the dog, so she adopted him and took him back to Washington.

Each December, the current president lights a National Christmas Tree located on the Ellipse, which is a beautiful lawn area directly behind the White House. Yuki, in a small Santa Claus suit, attended the ceremony with President Johnson in 1967.

Many exciting events occurred during the Johnson administration. In 1968 American astronauts flew several times around the moon and returned safely. Johnson honored them at a White House ceremony.

When the Johnsons went back home to Texas following his years in the White House, there was now time for Johnson to write his memoirs, operate the ranch and enjoy his family and friends. Lady Bird, too, was busy with her business concerns, her interests in wildflower conservation, in making a comfortable home for her husband, entertaining, and often visiting her married daughters, Luci (Mrs. Ian Turpin) and Lynda (Mrs. Charles Robb) and their grandchildren.

Yuki, too, retired to the ranch.

RICHARD M. NIXON

Thirty-seventh President.

President 1969 - 1974.

Born: Yorba Linda, California, January 9, 1913.

Richard Nixon was a top student at Whittier College and the Duke University Law School. He began the practice of law in a law firm in his home town of Whittier, California.

He was to marry lovely Patricia "Pat" Nixon. Patricia had worked very hard in her short life. She had lost her mother when only thirteen years old and had taken on the task of housekeeping for her father and two older brothers. Her father died when Pat was only 18 and she was on her own. Pat worked her way through the University of Southern California and became a teacher in Whittier, California.

She met attorney Richard Nixon in a Little Theater group. They were married in June 1940.

Nixon served in World War II in the Navy in the Pacific theater of war. After his military service he was elected to Congress and in 1950 he was elected to the Senate. Pat Nixon was tireless in working for her husband in his political career. Both were devoted to their two daughters, Patricia "Tricia" (later Mrs. Edward Cox) and Julie (later Mrs. David Eisenhower).

Dwight Eisenhower selected Nixon as his vice president. Later, in 1968, Nixon was nominated for president and was elected. There followed busy years in which he met many challenges. He ended the draft, ended the Vietnam War, and made new relationships with nations abroad, including China.

There were happy events at the White House. His beautiful daughter Tricia was married there. During his term of office United States astronauts were honored for making the first successful manned landings on the moon and returning safely to earth.

In 1972 Nixon was elected to serve a second term.

Checkers, a black, floppy-eared Cocker spaniel was a famous dog when Nixon was vice president but did not live long enough to become First Dog. The White House staff gave Nixon another dog, King Timahoe, in January 1969, for his birthday. King liked to ride with the president in his golf cart.

Julie had a miniature French poodle, Vicky. Trisha's dog was a Yorkshire terrier, Pasha. When the president and his family went to Florida for vacations, the dogs went along, too.

In 1972 it was front page news when the Premier of China gave President Nixon two giant pandas. Thousands of people have since come to the National Zoo to see these interesting animals.

Nixon's second term of office ended early with his resignation in August of 1974. Vice President Gerald Ford became president. Richard and Patricia Nixon retired to their home in San Clemente, California.

GERALD R. FORD

Thirty-eighth President.

President 1974 - 1977.

Born: Omaha, Nebraska, July 14, 1913.

When the Fords came to live in the White House they had only one pet, a Siamese cat called Shan. But before long a beautiful eight-month-old golden retriever was given to the president by his daughter seventeen-year-old Susan and the White House photographer, David Kennerly. The dog's name was Liberty.

Gerald "Jerry" Ford was raised in Grand Rapids, Michigan. He was born Leslie Lynch King. His mother and father were divorced when he was a baby. His mother, Dorothy, married again and his stepfather Gerald R. Ford adopted the little boy and gave him a new name.

In college Ford was a football star. He later earned his way through law school at Yale

University as a member of the athletic staff.

After several years of practicing law and serving in the Naval Reserve, Ford turned to politics. In 1948 he was elected to Congress and later became Republican minority leader of the House of Representatives.

The year 1948 was an important one in many ways for Gerald Ford. He married Elizabeth "Betty" Bloomer on October 15, 1948. Jerry and Betty had four children, Michael, John (Jack), Steven, and Susan. Betty Ford led a very busy life raising these children and coping with their projects and their pets, for her husband was often busy with Congressional business.

She was a charming and outspoken First Lady. The nation loved to hear about her life in the White House and about the Ford children. Susan Ford held her senior prom at the White House. Photographs of the attractive family and the family pets were often seen in magazines and newspaper articles. One, in 1975, shows the golden retriever Liberty and a litter of nine soft puppies being admired by Susan, Betty and President Ford.

The Fords donated one "pet" to the National Zoo in 1976, however, an elephant called Ashanti, from Sri Lanka.

After their White House years Gerald and Betty Ford retired to pursue their interests in business, sports and charities.

JAMES E. "JIMMY" CARTER

Thirty-Ninth President.

President 1977 - 1981.

Born: Plains, Georgia, October 1, 1924.

The Carter White House had its share of pets. Young Amy Carter saw to that. Jimmy and Rosalynn Carter had four children: John William, James Earl III, Donnel Jeffrey and Amy Lynn. Each was born in a different state thanks to Carter's seven years in the Navy.

Raised in the farming community of Plains, Georgia, Jimmy (James Earl Carter, Jr.) attended the United States Naval Academy and upon graduation in 1946 married Rosalynn Smith.

Carter went back to Plains after the death of his father and took part in the family business. He became interested in politics. Elected governor of Georgia, Carter stressed efficiency in government, ecological concerns and human rights.

Taking office as president in 1977, Carter and his family moved into the White House. The youngest Carter, Amy, treasured a cat called Misty-Melarky Ying-Yang. Also, her school teacher, Mrs. Verona Meeder of Lanham, Maryland, offered Amy a puppy and it was gladly adopted at the White House. (Amy attended a District of Columbia public school where Mrs. Meeder taught.) But the dog, Grits, eventually had to leave, never becoming "White-House broken."

As always, the office of president proved to be a demanding one. The president worked to increase jobs and stabilize the nation's economy. He was concerned over the nation's environmental matters. Carter expanded the national park system by some 103 million acres of Alaskan land.

This was a time when inflation and high interest rates were a problem. There were many international affairs to claim his attention. Again, pets helped the president to relax.

Having lost the election for a second term, the Carters returned to Plains, Georgia. They now work with the Carter Presidential Library in Atlanta and help with Habitat, an organization that is devoted to improving housing for lower income people in the United States and abroad.

Both Jimmy and Rosalynn Carter work to preserve the world environment and for better health for people around the world.

RONALD W. REAGAN

Fortieth President.

President 1981 - 1989.

Born: Tampico, Illinois, February 6, 1911.

After working his way through college, Ronald Reagan became a sports announcer and later a screen actor for twenty years. He married his first wife, Jane Wyman, and two children were born to them, Maureen and Michael. Reagan was a successful movie actor for many years. He married again in 1952 to Nancy Davis, and two children were born to them, Patricia and Ronald.

As president of the Screen Actors Guild, Reagan became interested in government and politics. In 1966 he was elected governor of California and was reelected in 1970. In 1980 Reagan was nominated for president and won the election. He served two terms as president. These were prosperous years. Reagan stressed strong defense forces and met with foreign leaders to help ease world tensions.

When Ronald and Nancy Reagan moved into the White House they set in motion extensive renovations of the second and third-floor living areas. As do many dedicated First Ladies, Nancy Reagan spent much of her time on worthy causes, for example, the fight against drug use.

Nancy liked to take Rex, her Cavalier King Charles spaniel, with her when she traveled to the Reagan ranch in California or to Camp David. (Camp David is a presidential retreat in the mountains of Maryland.) He was a Christmas gift to the Reagans in December 1985. In 1981 President Reagan had a dog called Lucky, a Bouvier Des Flanders. Lucky was a bouncy, big dog and movie footage shows her dragging the slender First Lady hither and yon. By Thanksgiving of 1985, Lucky was sent to live at the ranch in California, being too boisterous for the White House. Several other dogs lived at the ranch, so Lucky was not lonely.

The Reagans were pleased to get living gifts but passed many on to the National Zoo. Understandably, they did not keep an elephant from Sri Lanka, bald eagles from Germany, nor Israeli Dorcas gazelles and Fenner foxes. The zoo was very pleased to get from the White House six Nepalese/Indian gavials, a very rare, almost extinct, crocodile.

At his ranch, the president enjoyed riding his favorite horses. You might consider these pets — of the Western White House. The Reagans retired to their home in California.

GEORGE H. BUSH

Forty-first President.

President 1989 - 1993.

Born: Milton, Massachusetts, June 12, 1924.

Before George Herbert Walker Bush was elected president, his wife Barbara wrote a book narrated from the viewpoint of their dog, *C. Fred's Story,* "slightly edited by Barbara Bush." It was witty and funny and a best seller. The funds she realized from the book were donated to Mrs. Bush's favorite charities.

George Bush met Barbara Pierce when she was only sixteen years old, while they were both in college. A year-and-a-half later they were engaged. George Bush then left on tours of duty as a Navy fighter pilot. While he was back on leave in January of 1945, they were married.

Following the war, George graduated from Yale University and they went to Texas where

George was successful in the oil business. Six children were born: George, Pauline "Robin," John "Jeb", Neil, Marvin and Dorothy.

George turned to public service and politics and was often away from home. Barbara "kept the home fires burning." Sadness reached the family. George and Barbara to this day grieve the loss of their daughter, Robin (Pauline Robinson Bush), who died of leukemia in 1953, before she was four years old.

With their active children, and later, the grandchildren, Barbara and George were kept busy no matter where they lived.

For a time they lived in The People's Republic of China while George Bush was Chief of the U.S. Liaison Office there. Leaving China in 1974, C. Fred returned with the Bush family to the United States. There George served as Director of the Central Intelligence Agency.

During the eight years of the Reagan administration, George Bush served as vice president of the United States.

George Bush was elected president in 1988 and took office in 1989. When George and Barbara Bush moved into the White House, their children were grown but often came to see them. Also, the grandchildren were welcomed frequently. Mrs. Bush often said that she loved living in the White House. She enjoyed the beauty of the historic old mansion and appreciated the work of its devoted staff members. Barbara worked for literacy programs to help people learn to read. She continues to encourage young and old to read.

By the time the Bushs had come to the White House, C. Fred had passed away and First Dog was Millie (Mildred Kerr Bush)! Millie, an English Springer spaniel, got top press coverage when she gave birth to puppies. Mrs. Bush helped serve as mid-wife. One of the puppies, Ranger, returned later to become the president's dog.

Millie, too, was to pen her memoirs, *Millie's Book*, "as dictated to Barbara Bush," in 1990. Income from the book again was given to Mrs. Bush's charities. This book was a great success and is most entertaining.

Not all was smooth sailing for the First Dog. When the *Washingtonian* magazine selected Millie as the ugliest dog in Washington, Millie bit back. She is (said) to have said, according to a White House spokesperson, that this was "an arf-front" and that she has been a wonderful role model for dogs everywhere. Millie said that she had raised her family, doesn't stray from the yard and does her best to keep her master in line. "It's just not right to be hounded like this."

WILLIAM JEFFERSON "BILL" CLINTON

Forty-second President.

President 1993 -

Born: Hope Arkansas, August 19, 1946.

It was a beautiful day for a presidential inauguration. The sun shone, the temperatures, while nippy, were pleasant.

William Jefferson "Bill" Clinton arrived at the Capitol building with outgoing President Bush and Mrs. Bush. Bill's wife Hillary wore an attractive coat and hat that protected her from the cold. Chelsea, the Clinton's twelve-year-old daughter wore a warm coat and a delighted smile, as she was escorted onto the reviewing stand by a perfectly turned out military man. Her cloud of gold-brown hair helped protect her from the cold.

Family members, officials from the government, the Supreme Court, the House of Representatives and the Senate, attended the event.

Clinton opened his remarks with a tribute to President Bush, thanking him for his many years of public service. In less than an hour Bill Clinton was inaugurated as the forty-second president of the United States.

All around the world millions of people, suffering from war and civil unrest, marveled at the peaceful exchange of power demonstrated in the United States in that January inauguration.

Bill Clinton, a fifth generation Arkansan, was born William Jefferson Blyth, IV in 1946. Two months before his birth his father died in a traffic accident. After Bill was born his mother studied and worked hard to qualify for a position in nursing so that she could provide for herself and her son. He lived with his maternal grandparents while she attended nurses' training.

When he was four years old, his mother married Roger Clinton, a car dealer from Hot Springs. Roger Clinton adopted his wife's young son and so Bill's last name became Clinton. In the 1950's Roger Clinton, Bill's half-brother, was born.

You might almost say that Bill Clinton had been preparing and studying for the job as president all his life. He worked hard in school, took part in school activities and got good grades. In 1968 he received a Bachelor's degree from

Georgetown University. He then spent two years at Oxford University in England as a Rhodes Scholar. Next he earned a law degree from Yale University's Law School in 1973.

While at Yale, Clinton met a lovely young woman, blonde, intelligent, Hillary Rodham. In 1975 they were married. They both had careers in Little Rock, Arkansas, where they had gone to live after university. In 1981 a daughter was born to them and named Chelsea.

Among his many posts and honors Bill Clinton is perhaps best known as only the second person in Arkansas history to be elected to five terms as governor of that state. While governor, he pushed through legislation benefiting education, ably assisted by his wife Hillary.

Today, President Clinton often goes out to jog in the morning before getting to work in the Oval Office. He enjoys golf and also likes to play his saxophone.

All of this is fascinating, but what of pets? "Socks" is the answer. Chelsea's cat "Socks" became an overnight celebrity when Clinton was chosen to run for president. Photographers stalked Socks and his picture appeared in magazines and newspapers. The little black animal has amber eyes, white markings and, as his name indicates, four white socks.

How did the Clintons get Socks? A few

years ago Chelsea had a dog called Zeke, but Zeke died and Chelsea grieved for him. One day, while still living in Little Rock, Hillary and Chelsea learned that Chelsea's music teacher had taken in two stray kittens. Both Hillary and Bill Clinton are allergic to cats, but they believed that their daughter needed a pet, so Socks was adopted.

Little did Socks think, as a kitten, that he would one day become First Cat. (Actually, cats don't worry about titles, they just like to be near humans who are devoted to them.)

Cats are smart and rather slippery customers, so when Socks came to Washington, he had to be taken outside on a long leash. Cats need time to become accustomed to a new home and the Clintons did not want him setting out for Arkansas!

BIBLIOGRAPHY

Blassingame, Wyatt. *The Look-It-Up Book of Presidents*. New York: Random House, 1988.

Bourne, Miriam Anne. *White House Children*. New York: Random House, 1979.

Bryant, Traphes and Frances Spatz Leighton. *Dog Days at the White House*. New York: Macmillan Publishing Co., 1975.

Bush, Barbara. *C. Fred's Story: A Dog's Life*. "By C. Fred Bush, edited slightly by Barbara Bush." Garden City, NY: Doubleday & Company, Inc., 1984.

Bush, Barbara. *Millie's Book*. "As Dictated to Barbara Bush." New York: William Morrow, 1990.

Bush, George. *Looking Forward: An Autobiography*. New York: Doubleday, 1987.

Freidel, Frank. *Presidents of the United States*. Washington, D.C.: White House Historical Association, 1989.

James, Maquis. *Andrew Jackson: The Border Captain*. New York: Grosset and Dunlap, 1933.

Klapthor, Margaret Brown. *The First Ladies*. Washington, D.C.: White House Historical Association with the cooperation of the National Geographic Society, 1989.

Laskas, Jeanne Marie.   "Cats," *The Washington Post Magazine*, February 28, 1993.

Mergen, Alexa. *From Bison to Biopark: 100 Years of the National Zoo.* Washington, D.C.: Friends of the National Zoo, 1989.

Sandberg, Peter Lars. *Dwight D. Eisenhower.* New York: Chelsea House Publishers, 1986.

Seale, William. *The President's House: A History.* Two volumes. Washington, D.C.: The White House Historical Association with the National Geographic Society and Harry N. Abrams, Inc., 1986.

terHorst, J. F. *Gerald Ford and the Future of the Presidency.* New York, The Third Press, 1974.

Truman, Margaret. *White House Pets.* New York: David McKay Company, 1969.

Viola, Herman J. *Andrew Jackson.* New York: Chelsea House Publishers, 1986.

Ward, John William. *Andrew Jackson — Symbol for an Age.* New York: Oxford University Press, 1955.

Whitney, David C. *The American Presidents.* New York: Prentice Hall Press, 7th edition, revised and updated by Robin Vaughan Whitney, 1990.

Yang, John E. "A 1040 Form Signed With A Pawprint," *The Washington Post*, April 16, 1992, A21.

ABOUT THE AUTHOR

Born in North Carolina to attorney Joseph M. Prevette and his wife Hilda Graf Prevette, the author grew up dreaming of becoming a writer, of piloting aircraft, of marriage and children.

In Florida in the 1940s she learned to fly and began flight instructing. She continues to hold a pilot's license.

In 1949, she married and wrote for a national aviation magazine in Washington, D.C.

Later she and her husband and their two children moved to Maryland. It was in the 1960s that she began to write about Maryland topics and established the Maryland Historical Press. At the same time, she began work toward a degree a the University of Maryland. Thirty years later she had earned a B.A. in American History; an M.A. in American History; and a Ph.D. in Education Development, Policy and Administration (1991).

During these thirty years, the author married again and continued to operate the publishing company. As Vera Foster Rollo, in the late 1970s she served as Associate Professor of History and coordinator of the Aviation Studies Program at Wilmington College, New Castle, Delaware. Returning to Maryland she wrote and published college-level texts on aviation law. Then, filling a need, wrote books on American history.

Dr. Rollo followed her work as a flight instructor with active duty in the Civil Air Patrol. She has made several trips to Europe to research American colonial era subjects. She now lives in Maryland where she publishes books by several noted authors; enjoys gardening and the company of several dogs. She takes time out to visit her daughter, Sally, in Atlanta and her son, Michael, and his family in San Francisco.

INDEX